**worship
BAND
PLAY-ALONG**

KEYBOARD EDITION *Volume 1*

Holy Is the Lord

Recorded and produced by Jim Reith at BeatHouse Music, Milwaukee, WI

Lead Vocals by Tonia Emrich and Jim Reith
Background Vocals by Jim Reith and Jana Wolf
Guitars by Mike DeRose
Bass by Chris Kringel
Piano by Kurt Cowling
Drums by Del Bennett

ISBN 13: 978-1-4234-1712-5
ISBN 10: 1-4234-1712-7

HAL•LEONARD®
CORPORATION
7777 W. BLUEMOUND RD. P.O. BOX 13819 MILWAUKEE, WI 53213

Visit Hal Leonard Online at
www.halleonard.com

Holy Is the Lord

Agnus Dei

Words and Music by Michael W. Smith

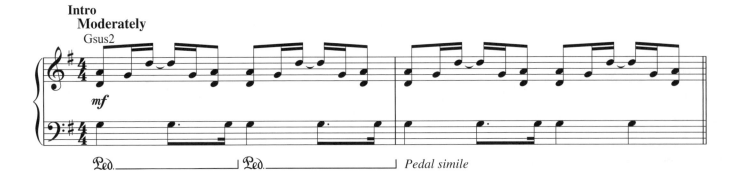

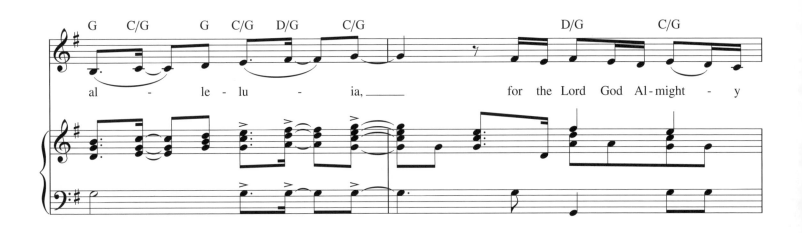

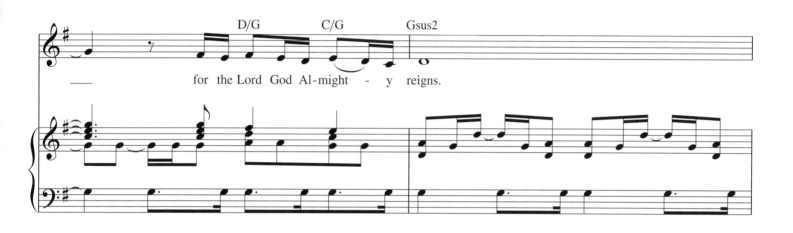

Chorus 1

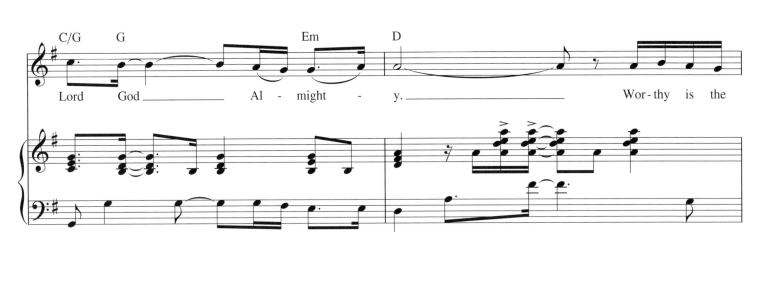

Lord God _____ Al - might - y. _____ Wor - thy is the

Lamb, _____ wor - thy is the Lamb. A -

men. _____ Al - le - lu - ia, ____

____ al - le - lu - ia, ____

for the Lord God Al-might - y reigns.

Al - le - lu - ia, _____

al - le - lu - ia, _____ for the Lord God Al-might - y

reigns. Al - le - lu - ia. _

Chorus 2

Ho - ly, _____ Ho -

ly _____ are You, Lord God _____ Al - might -

y. _____ Wor-thy is the Lamb, _____ wor-thy is the

Lamb. You are ho - ly, _____ ho -

Be Unto Your Name

Words and Music by Lynn DeShazo and Gary Sadler

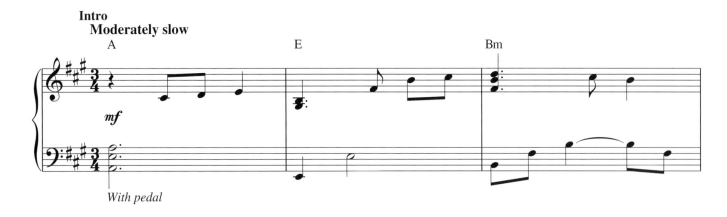

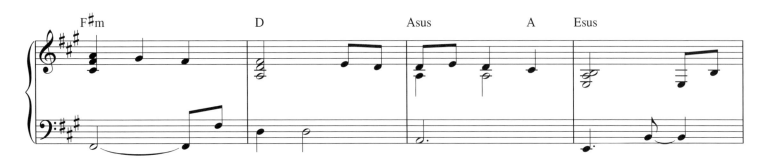

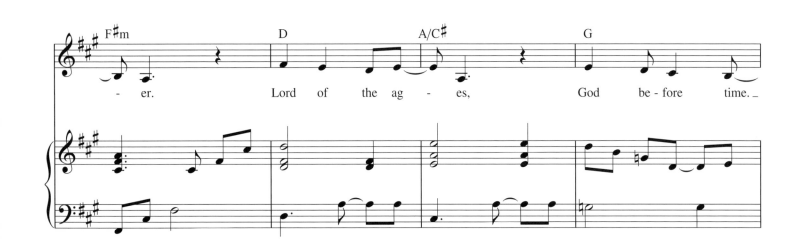

You are the heal - er. Jesus, Re - deem - er,

might - y to save. ___ You are the love ___ song

we'll sing for - ev - er, bow - ing be - fore ___ You,

bless - ing Your name. _____ Ho - ly,

Chorus

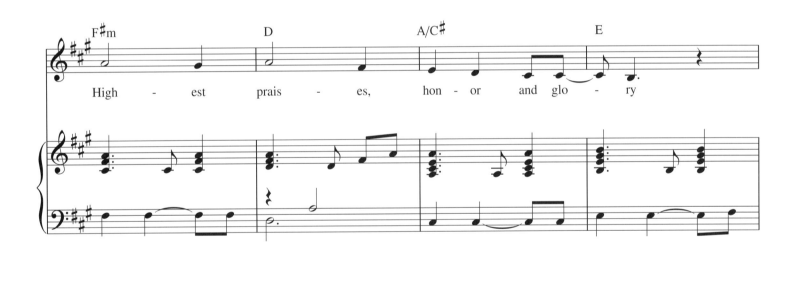

Bm   F♯m   Esus   E

be un - to Your name.

Chorus

F♯m   D   A/C♯   E

Ho - ly, ho - ly, Lord God Al - might - y,

p

F♯m   D   A   E

Wor - thy is the Lamb who was slain.

f

F♯m   D   A/C♯   E

High - est prais - es, hon - or and glo - ry

Open the Eyes of My Heart

Words and Music by Paul Baloche

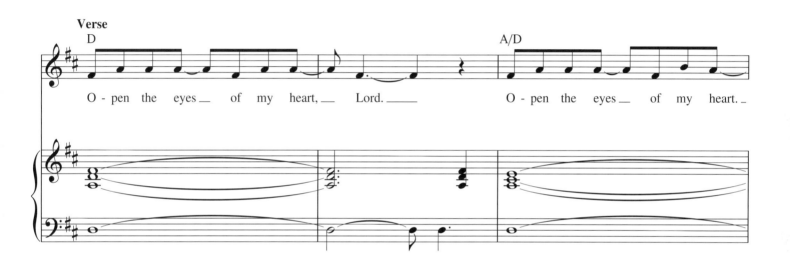

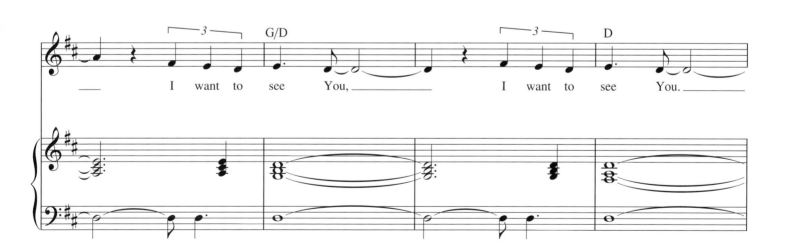

ho - ly, ho - ly, ho - ly, _____ I want to see You. _____

Tag

_____ I want to see You, _____ I want to

see You, _____ I want to see You, __ oh, _____

I want to see You. _____

God of Wonders

Words and Music by Marc Byrd and Steve Hindalong

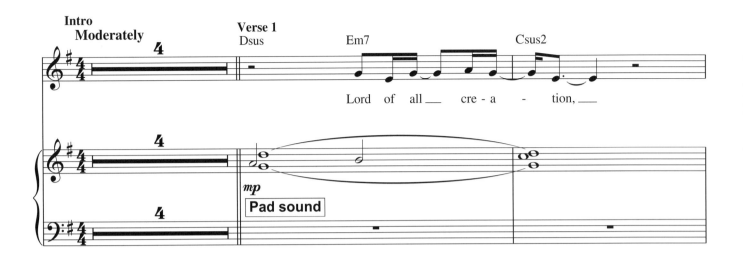

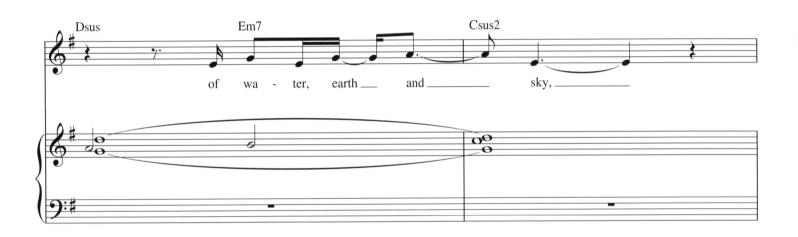

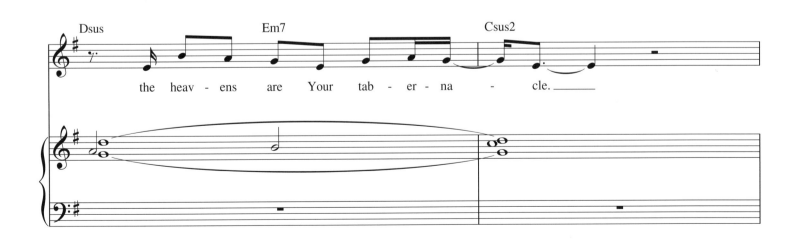

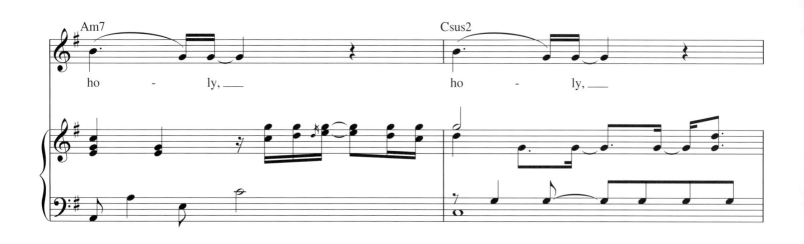

ho - ly, ___ ho - ly, ___

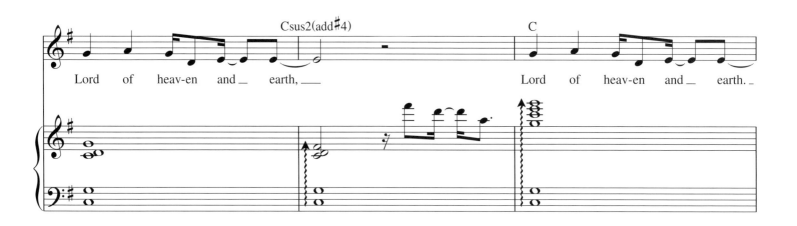

Lord of heav-en and ___ earth, ___ Lord of heav-en and ___ earth. _

Verse 2

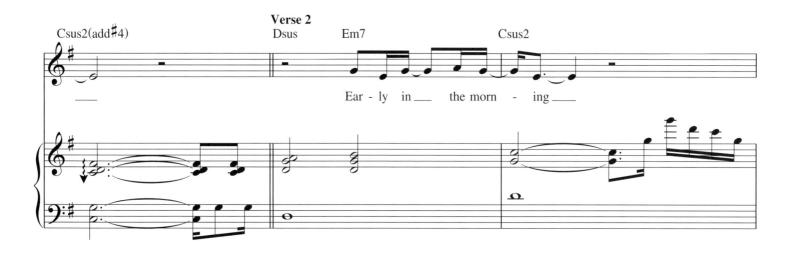

___ Ear - ly in ___ the morn - ing ___

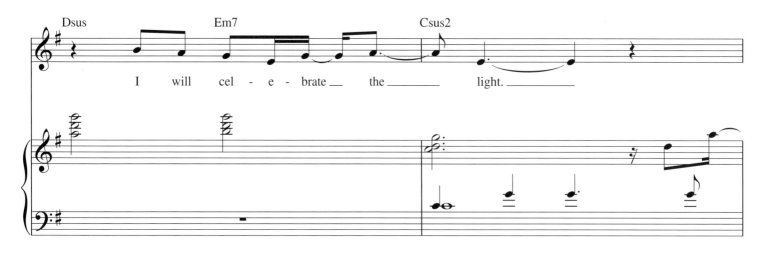

I will cel - e - brate ___ the ___ light. ___

un - i - verse _ de - clares Your maj - es - ty. You are

ho - ly, _____ ho - ly, _____

Bridge

Hal - le - lu - jah to the Lord _____ of _____ heav - en and _____ earth. _____

_____ Hal - le - lu - jah to the Lord _____ of _____ heav - en and _____ earth. _____

Holy Is the Lord

Words and Music by Chris Tomlin and Louie Giglio

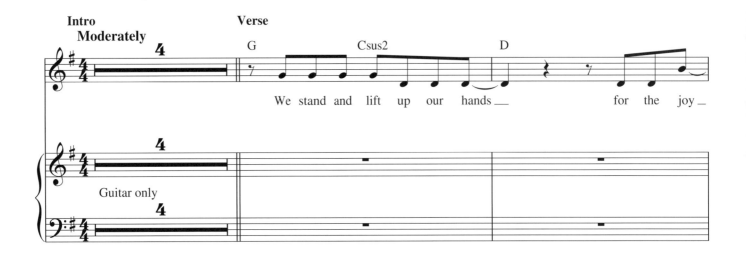

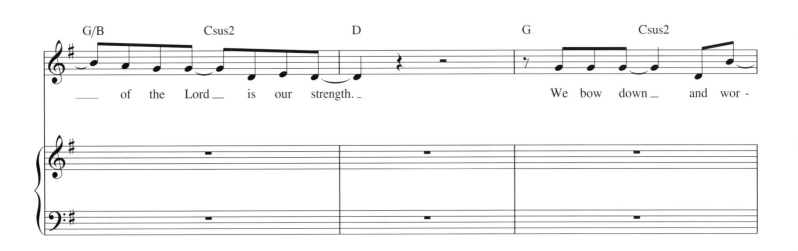

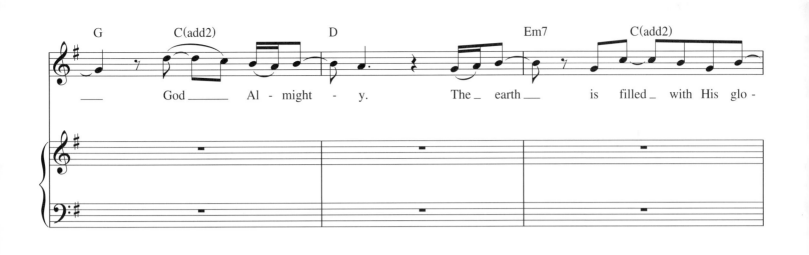

God _____ Al - might - y. The _ earth ___ is filled _ with His glo -

Chorus

- ry. Ho - ly is the Lord ___ God _____ Al - might -

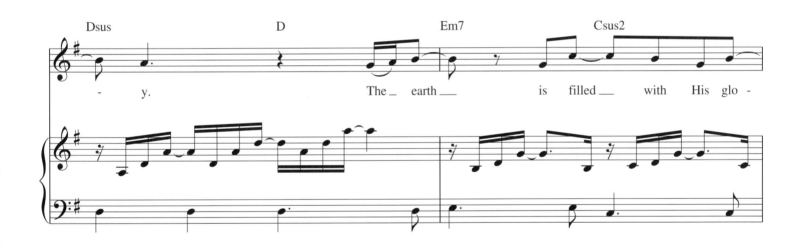

- y. The _ earth ___ is filled ___ with His glo -

- ry. Ho - ly is the Lord ___ God _____ Al - might -

It Is You

Words and Music by Peter Furler

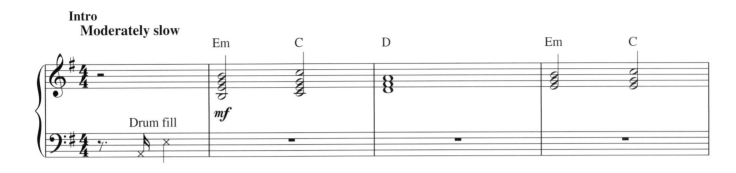

As we lift up our hands, ___ will You meet us here? ___

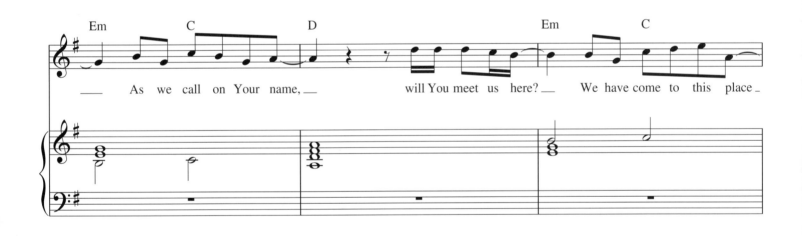

___ As we call on Your name, ___ will You meet us here? ___ We have come to this place ___

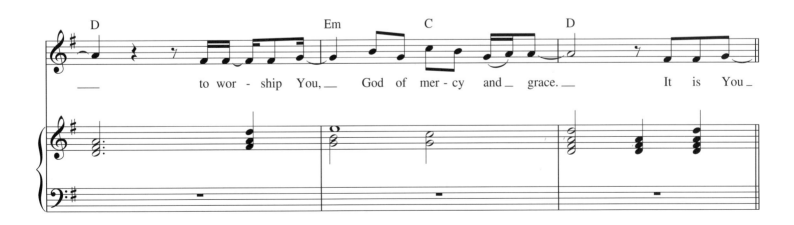

___ to wor - ship You, ___ God of mer - cy and ___ grace. ___ It is You ___

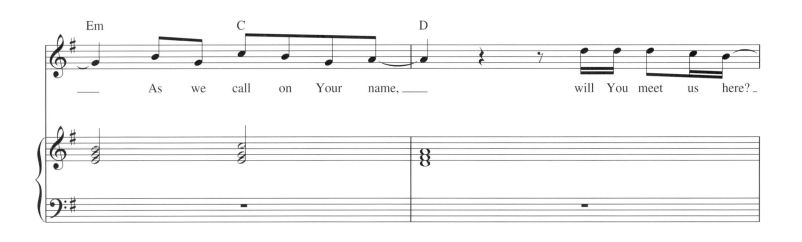

As we call on Your name, ____ will You meet us here? _

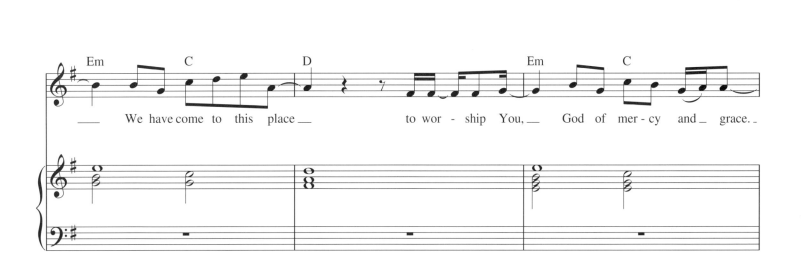

____ We have come to this place ____ to wor-ship You, ____ God of mer-cy and ____ grace. _

Pre-Chorus

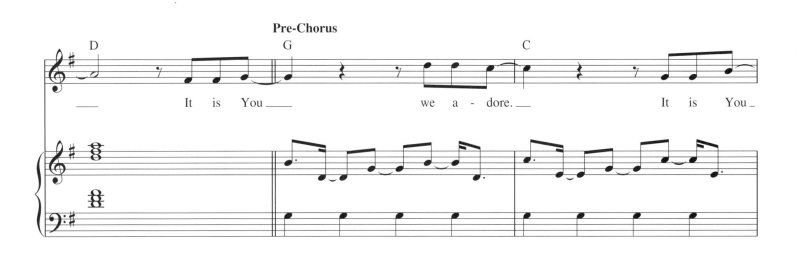

____ It is You ____ we a-dore. ____ It is You _

____ prais-es are for. ____ On-ly You ____ the heav-ens de-clare. _

Chorus

And ho - ly, ho - ly is our ___ God Al - might - y ___

and ho - ly, ho - ly is His ___ name a - lone. ___

And ho - ly, ho - ly is our ___ God Al - might - y ___

We Fall Down

Words and Music by Chris Tomlin

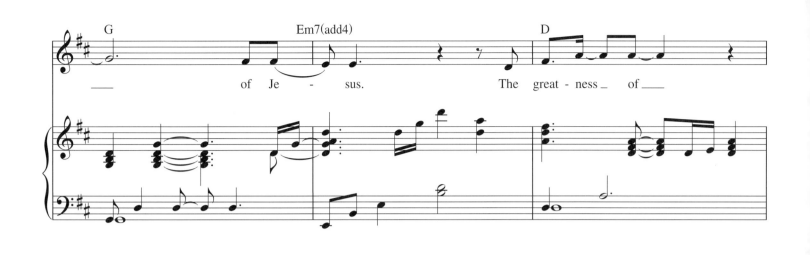

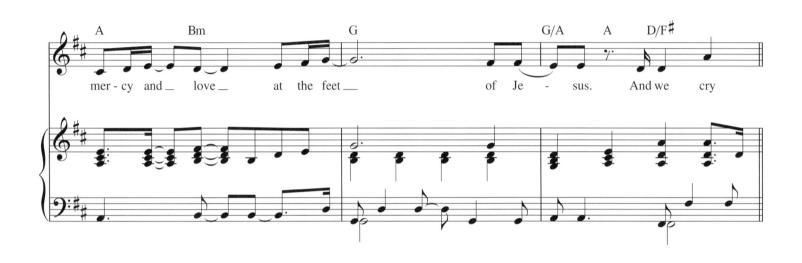

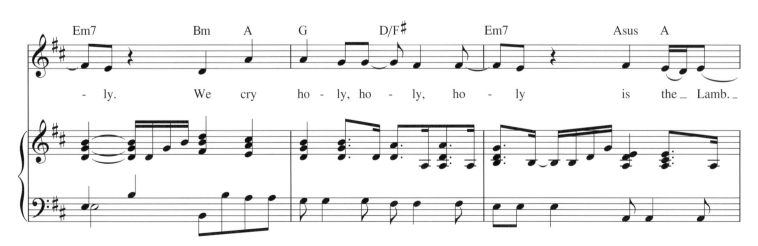

You Are Holy
(Prince of Peace)

Words and Music by Marc Imboden and Tammi Rhoton

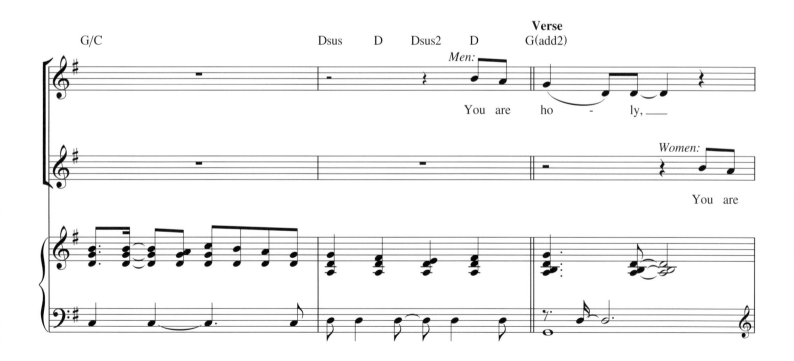

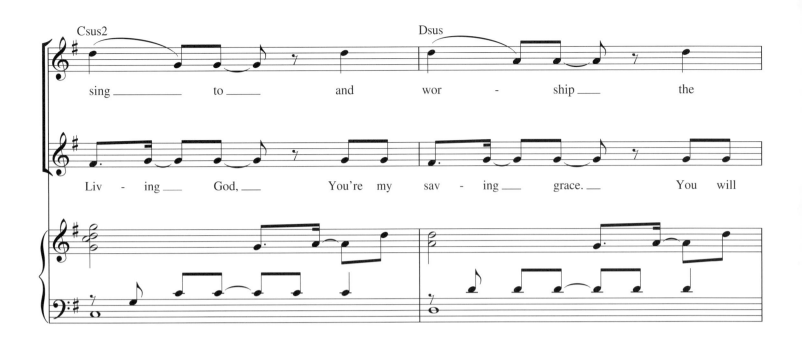

sing _____ to _____ and wor - ship _____ the

Liv - ing _____ God, _____ You're my sav - ing _____ grace. _____ You will

King _____ who ___ is wor - thy. And I will love _____ and ___ a -

reign for - ev - er, You are An - cient ___ of Days. You are Al - pha, O - me - ga, Be -

dore _____ Him, _____ and I will bow _____ down _____ be -

gin - ning and ___ End. You're my Sav - ior, Mes - si - ah, Re -

AGNUS DEI

MICHAEL W. SMITH

Key of **G Major**, 4/4

VERSE:

Gsus2 G   C/G G C/G   G
       Al   - le - lu - ia

G   C/G G C/G D/G C/G
Al - le - lu - ia

      D/G   C/G   G
For the Lord God Almighty reigns

G C/G G C/G   G
Al - le - lu - ia

G C/G G C/G D/G C/G
Al - le - lu - ia

      D/G   C/G   G
For the Lord God Almighty reigns

G C/G G C/G D/G C/G
Al - le - lu - ia

CHORUS 1:

C/G   D/F# G
Ho -   ly

D/F#   G(add2)
Ho - ly

        C/G G   Em   D
Are You, Lord God Almight - y

        C(add2)
Worthy is the Lamb

        C
Worthy is the Lamb

C   D Gsus2
A - men

(REPEAT VERSE)

CHORUS 2:

C/E D/G G
Ho - ly

D/G   G
Ho - ly

        C/G G   Em   D
Are You, Lord God Almight - y

        C(add2)
Worthy is the Lamb

        C(add2)
Worthy is the Lamb

        G
You are ho - ly

D/G   G
Ho - ly

        C/G G   Em   D
Are You, Lord God Almight - y

        C
Worthy is the Lamb

        C
Worthy is the Lamb

C   D Gsus2
A - men

BE UNTO YOUR NAME

LYNN DESHAZO and GARY SADLER

Key of **A Major, 3/4**

INTRO:

A E Bm F♯m D Asus A Esus E

VERSE 1:

A   E   Bm   F♯m
We are a moment, You are forever

D   A/C#   G   E
Lord of the ages,   God before time

A   E   Bm   F♯m
We are a vapor, You are eternal

D   A/C♯   G   Esus   E
Love everlasting, reigning on high

CHORUS:

F♯m D   A/C♯   A
Holy, Holy, Lord God Almighty

F♯m   D   A   E
Worthy is the Lamb who was slain

F♯m   D   A/C♯   E
Highest praises, honor and glory

Bm   F♯m   Esus   E
    Be unto Your name

Bm   F♯m   Esus   E
    Be unto Your name

VERSE 2:

A   E   Bm   F♯m
We are the broken, You are the healer

D   A/C♯   G   E
Jesus, Redeemer, mighty to save

A   E   Bm   F♯m
You are the love song we'll sing forever

D   A/C♯   G   Esus   E
Bowing before You, blessing Your name.

(REPEAT CHORUS 2X)

TAG:

Bm   F♯m   Esus   E
    Be unto   Your name

Bm   F♯m   Esus   E (hold)
    Be unto   Your name

GOD OF WONDERS

MARC BYRD and STEVE HINDALONG

Key of **G Major**, 4/4

VERSE 1:

Dsus Em7   Csus2
Lord of all creation

Dsus   Em   Csus2
Of water, earth and sky

Dsus   Em   Csus2
The heavens are Your tabernacle

Dsus   Em   Csus2
Glory to the Lord on high

CHORUS:

G   Dsus D
God of wonders beyond our galaxy

       Am7   Csus2
You are holy, holy

   G   Dsus D
The universe declares Your majesty

       Am7   Csus2
You are holy,   holy

Csus2   Csus2(add#4)
Lord of heaven and earth

C   Csus2(add#4)
Lord of heaven and earth

VERSE 2:

Dsus Em7   Csus2
Early in the morning

Dsus   Em   Csus2
I will celebrate the light

Dsus Em7   C
And as I stumble in the darkness

Dsus   Em7   Csus2
I will call Your name by night

(REPEAT CHORUS)

BRIDGE:

Am7   Cmaj7
Hallelujah to the Lord of heaven and earth

Am7   Cmaj7
Hallelujah to the Lord of heaven and earth

Am7   Cmaj7
Hallelujah to the Lord of heaven and earth

Am7   Cmaj7
Hallelujah to the Lord of heaven and earth

Dsus   D

CHORUS:

G   Dsus D
God of wonders beyond our galaxy

       Am7   Csus2
You are holy, holy

   G   Dsus D
The universe declares Your majesty

       Am7   Csus2
You are holy,   holy

Csus2   Csus2(add#4)
Lord of heaven and earth

C   Csus2(add#4)
Lord of heaven and earthC

C(add2)   Csus2(add#4)
Lord of heaven and earth

HOLY IS THE LORD

CHRIS TOMLIN and LOUIE GIGLIO

Key of **G Major, 4/4**

INTRO (GUITAR ONLY):

G   Csus2   D

G   Csus2   D

VERSE:

G   Csus2   D
We stand and lift up our hands

      G/B   Csus2   D
For the joy of the Lord is our strength

G   Csus2   D
We bow down and worship Him now

G/B   Csus2   D
How great, how awesome is He

        A7sus   Csus2
Together we sing

CHORUS:

      G/B Csus2 Dsus D
Holy is the Lord God Almighty

   Em7   Csus2   Dsus
The earth is filled with His glory

D   G/B Csus2 Dsus D
Holy is the Lord God Almighty

   Em7   Csus2   Dsus D
The earth is filled with His glory

   Em7   Csus2   Dsus D
The earth is filled with His glory

(REPEAT VERSE & CHORUS)

BRIDGE:

   G   D/F♯
It's rising up all around

          F   C
It's the anthem of the Lord's renown

   G   D/F♯
It's rising up all around

          F   C
It's the anthem of the Lord's renown

               A7sus   Cadd2
And together we sing

         A7sus   Cadd2
Everyone sing

(REPEAT CHORUS)

(REPEAT LAST LINE OF CHORUS)

END ON G

IT IS YOU

PETER FURLER

Key of **G Major**, 4/4

INTRO:

Em C D   Em C D

VERSE:

Em   C   D
As we lift up our hands, will You meet us here

Em   C   D
As we call on Your name, will You meet us here

Em   C   D
We have come to this place to worship You

Em   C   D
God of mercy and grace

PRE-CHORUS:

   G   C
It is You we adore

   G   C
It is You praises are for

   G   C
Only You the heavens declare

   G   C
It is You, it is You

CHORUS:

D   C   G
And holy, holy is our God Almighty

D   C   G
And holy, holy is His name alone

D   C   G
And holy, holy is our God Almighty

D   C   G
And holy, holy is His name alone

TRANSITION BACK TO VERSE:

   G   C
It is You we adore

       G   C
It is You, only You

(REPEAT VERSE, PRE-CHORUS & CHORUS)

BRIDGE:

G   D
As we lift up our hands

      C   G
As we call on Your name

          D
Will You visit this place

      C   G
By Your mercy and grace

      D
As we lift up our hands

      C   G
As we call on Your name

          D
Will You visit in this place

      C   G
By Your mercy and grace

G   C
It is You we adore

   G   C
It is You, it is You

(REPEAT CHORUS 2X)

ENDING:

   G   C
It is You we adore

   G   C (hold)
It is You, only You

OPEN THE EYES OF MY HEART

PAUL BALOCHE

Key of **D Major**, 4/4

INTRO (FOUR BARS):

Dsus2

VERSE:

D
Open the eyes of my heart, Lord

A/D
Open the eyes of my heart

       G/D
I want to see You

       D
I want to see You

(REPEAT VERSE)

CHORUS:

         A   **Bm**
To see You high and lifted up

G   **A**
Shining in the light of Your glory

A   **Bm**
Pour out Your power and love

        G   **A**
As we sing holy, holy, holy

(REPEAT VERSE 2X)

(REPEAT CHORUS 2X)

VERSE (2X):

D
Holy, holy holy

A/C♯
Holy, holy, holy

G/B   **G**
Holy, holy, holy

        D
I want to see You

TAG (2X):

D/F♯   **G**   **D**
I want to see You, I want to see You

WE FALL DOWN

CHRIS TOMLIN

Key of **D Major, 4/4**

INTRO (FOUR BARS):

D   A Bm G(add2)

VERSE:

D   A   Bm
We fall down, we lay our crowns
         G   Em7(add4)
At the feet of Jesus
         D   A   Bm
The greatness of mercy and love
         G   G/A   A
At the feet of Jesus

CHORUS:

     D/F♯   G   D/F♯ Em7
And we cry holy, holy, holy

D/F♯   G   D/F♯ Em7
We cry holy, holy, holy

Bm A G   D/F♯ Em7
We cry holy, holy, holy

Asus D Dsus A Bm
Is the Lamb

G(add2) Em7(add4)

(REPEAT VERSE)

CHORUS:

     D/F♯   G   D/F♯ Em7
And we cry holy, holy, holy

D/F♯   G   D/F♯ Em7
We cry holy, holy, holy

Bm A G   D/F♯ Em7
We cry holy, holy, holy

Asus A D   Dsus D
Is   the Lamb

CHORUS:

Em7   D/F♯ G   D/F♯ Em7
And we cry   holy, holy, holy

D/F♯   G   D/F♯ Em7
We cry holy, holy, holy

Bm A G   D/F♯ Em7
We cry holy, holy, holy

Asus A D
Is   the Lamb

A Bm G Asus A D

© 1998 WORSHIPTOGETHER.COM SONGS (ASCAP)
Admin. by EMI CMG PUBLISHING
All Rights Reserved   Used by Permission

YOU ARE HOLY (PRINCE OF PEACE)

MARC IMBODEN and TAMMI RHOTON

Key of **G Major**, 4/4

INTRO (EIGHT BARS):

G   G/C   Dsus D Dsus2 D

G   G/C   Dsus D Dsus2 D

VERSE:

     G(add2)   *Echo:*
You are holy   *(You are holy)*

     C(add2)
You are mighty *(You are mighty)*

   Am7
You are worthy *(You are worthy)*

     D
Worthy of praise *(worthy of praise)*

   G(add2)
I will follow   *(I will follow)*

   C(add2)2
I will listen   *(I will listen)*

   Am7
I will love You *(I will love You)*

D   **G**   **D**   **G**
All of my days *(all of my days)*

CHORUS

(Part I and Part II sung simultaneously):

PART I

   Csus2   **Dsus**
I will sing to and worship

   Em7   **G/B**
The King who is worthy

     Csus2   **Dsus**
And I will love and adore Him

     Em7   **G/B**
And I will bow down before Him

     Csus2   **Dsus**
And I will sing to and worship

   Em7   **G/B**
The King who is worthy

     Csus2   **Dsus**
And I will love and adore Him

   Em7   **Asus** **A**
And I will bow down before Him

     C(add2)
You're my Prince of Peace

     D   **G**
And I will live my life for You.

(REPEAT VERSE)

(REPEAT CHORUS 2X)

TAG:

     Csus2
You're my Prince of Peace

      D   **G**
And I will live my life for You

PART II

     Csus2   **Dsus**
You are Lord of lords, You are King of kings

   Em7   **G/B**
You are mighty God, Lord of everything

     Csus2   **D**
You're Emmanuel, You're the Great I AM

     Em7   **G/B**
You're the Prince of Peace, who is the Lamb

     Csus2   **Dsus**
You're the Living God, You're my saving grace

     Em7   **G/B**
You will reign forever, You are Ancient of Days

     Csus2   **Dsus**
You are Alpha, Omega, Beginning and End

     Em7   **Asus**   **A**
You're my Savior, Messiah, Redeemer and Friend

     C(add2)
You're my Prince of Peace

     D   **G**
And I will live my life for You

The Best Sacred Collections for Piano

Lee Evans Arranges
BEAUTIFUL HYMNS AND SPIRITUALS
New interpretations of 12 of the world's most beautiful hymns and spirituals ever written. Songs include: The Wayfaring Stranger • Fairest Lord Jesus • Amazing Grace • Nearer, My God, To Thee • Rock of Ages.
00009635 Piano Solo $6.95

BEST-LOVED HYMNS
Dan Fox Easy Piano
37 sacred songs, including: Amazing Grace • Faith of Our Fathers • Just a Closer Walk with Thee • Onward, Christian Soldiers • Rock of Ages • Whispering Hope • and more.
00364196 Easy Piano $5.95

CHRISTIAN CHILDREN'S FAVORITES
arranged by Phillip Keveren
Excellent solo arrangements for beginning pianists of 24 Sunday School favorites: All Things Bright and Beautiful • The B-I-B-L-E • Do Lord • Down in My Heart • God Is So Good • He's Got the Whole World in His Hands • If You're Happy and You Know It • Jesus Loves Me • This Little Light of Mine • and more.
00310837 Beginning Piano Solos $10.95

CONTEMPORARY CHRISTIAN CLASSICS
12 timeless duets: Be Still and Know • Behold the Lamb • El Shaddai • Great Is the Lord • How Majestic Is Your Name • I've Just Seen Jesus • More Than Wonderful • People Need the Lord • Proclaim the Glory of the Lord • Upon This Rock • We Are So Blessed • We Shall Behold Him.
00240980 Piano Duet $8.95

CONTEMPORARY CHRISTIAN PIANO SOLOS
Piano solo arrangements of 17 contemporary Christian favorites, including: Friends • Great Is the Lord • People Need the Lord • Via Dolorosa • and more.
00294008 Piano Solo $9.95

EASY WAYS TO PRAISE
15 gospel and Contemporary Christian favorites: As the Deer • Awesome God • Bless His Holy Name • Great Is the Lord • He Is Exalted • I Love You Lord • Majesty • and more!
00310165 Easy Piano $8.95

"HOW BEAUTIFUL" & OTHER CONTEMPORARY CHRISTIAN FAVORITES
15 songs, including: Awesome God • Friends • Great Is the Lord • How Beautiful • In His Presence • Jubilaté • Majesty • People Need the Lord • Thank You • and more.
00310109 Big-Note Piano $8.95

THE LORD'S PRAYER & OTHER FAVORITE SACRED CLASSICS
arr. Bill Boyd • G. Schirmer, Inc.
A terrific collection of the most enduring and beloved sacred music, including Albert Hay Malotte's "The Lord's Prayer," plus: He Shall Feed His Flock • I Wonder as I Wander • Sheep May Safely Graze • Panis Angelicus • and more.
50481090 Easy Piano $7.95

PIANO PRAISE
arr. Jeff Bennett • Integrity Music & Hal Leonard
8 songs for performing in church as a soloist or at home for personal worship. Includes optional instrumental obbligato parts, chord symbols for improvisation, and a CD with play-along tracks and demonstrations.
08739851 Piano Solo (Book/CD Pack) $19.95

PRAISE & WORSHIP FAVORITES
8 arrangements that even beginners can enjoy, including: Ancient of Days • Breathe • Change My Heart, Oh God • Come, Now Is the Time to Worship • Here I Am to Worship • Open the Eyes of My Heart • Shine, Jesus, Shine • There Is None like You.
00311271 Beginning Piano Solo $9.95

PRAISEHYMNS
by Susan Naylor Callaway
This collection features medleys of beloved hymns and choruses, including: All Hail King Jesus/All Hail the Power of Jesus' Name • As the Deer/O Worship the King • He Is Exalted/Praise Him! Praise Him! • There Is a Redeemer/ When I Survey the Wondrous Cross • and more.
00310743 Piano Solo $10.95

SHOUT TO THE LORD!
arranged by Phillip Keveren
14 praise song favorites, including: El Shaddai • Great Is the Lord • How Beautiful • More Precious Than Silver • Oh Lord, You're Beautiful • Shout to the Lord • Thy Word • and more.
00310699 Piano Solo $12.95

TIMELESS PRAISE
arranged by Phillip Keveren
20 songs of worship: As the Deer • Give Thanks • How Majestic Is Your Name • Lord, I Lift Your Name on High • Oh Lord, You're Beautiful • People Need the Lord • Shine, Jesus, Shine • There Is a Redeemer • and more.
00310712 Easy Piano $12.95

TOP CHRISTIAN HITS
14 of today's hottest CCM hits arranged for easy piano. Includes: Blessed Be Your Name (Tree63) • Dare You to Move (Switchfoot) • Gone (tobyMac) • Holy Is the Lord (Chris Tomlin) • Much of You (Steven Curtis Chapman) • more!
00311263 Easy Piano $12.95

FOR MORE INFORMATION, SEE YOUR LOCAL MUSIC DEALER, OR WRITE TO:

HAL•LEONARD® CORPORATION

7777 W. BLUEMOUND RD. P.O. BOX 13819 MILWAUKEE, WI 53213

Visit our web site at **www.halleonard.com** for complete songlists and a listing of all products available.

0406

Prices, contents and availability subject to change without notice.